S.S. 142.]   [O.B. 147

PROVISIONAL NOTES ON FIRING AT AIRCRAFT WITH MACHINE GUNS AND OTHER SMALL ARMS.

ISSUED BY THE GENERAL STAFF.

March, 1917.

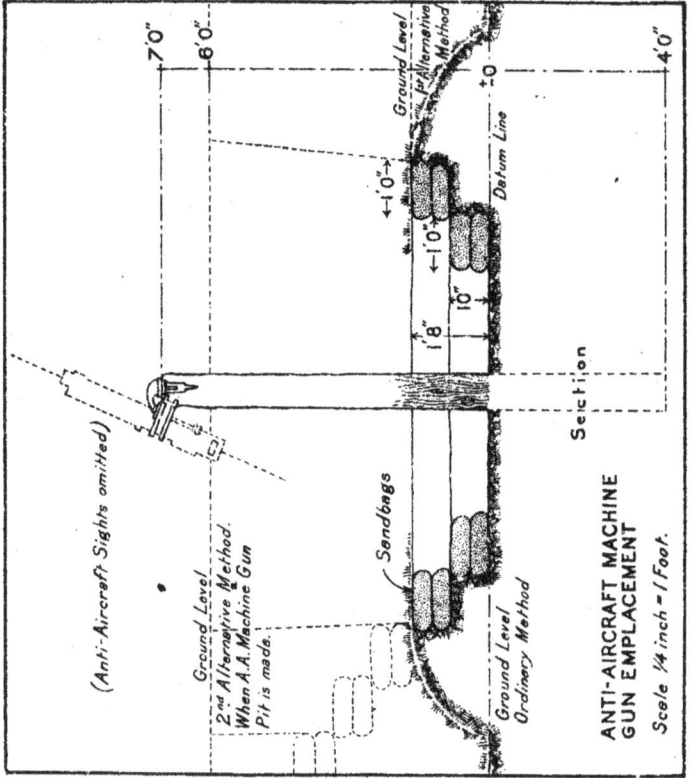

(Anti-Aircraft Sights omitted)

7'0"

6'0"

4'0"

Ground Level
1st Alternative
Method

Ground Level

Datum Line

±0

1'0"

1'0"

10"

1'8"

Section

Ground Level
2nd Alternative Method.
When A.A. Machine Gun
Pit is made.

Sandbags

Ground Level
Ordinary Method

ANTI-AIRCRAFT MACHINE
GUN EMPLACEMENT

Scale ¼ inch = 1 Foot.

PROVISIONAL NOTES ON FIRING AT AIRCRAFT WITH MACHINE GUNS AND OTHER SMALL ARMS.

CHIEF CONSIDERATIONS.

The difficulty of introducing an effective method of engaging aircraft from the ground with small arms is due to the number of factors which have to be considered, of these the following are some of the most important :—

(*a*) AFFECTING THE SIGHTING ELEVATION.—The distance of the aircraft from the gun—this affects the time of flight of the bullet, and therefore the trajectory of the bullet, and hence the sighting elevation of the gun.

The angle of sight—this affects the trajectory of the bullet (which becomes straighter as the angle of sight increases), and entails modification of the sighting elevation.

The direction of flight of the aircraft (which may or may not move in the same horizontal plane)—this quickly changes the distance and the angle of sight, and therefore the sighting elevation.

(*b*) AFFECTING DEFLECTION.—The speed of the aircraft—this may vary in still air from about 60 to 100 miles per hour and will probably increase in the near future.

The speed of the aircraft and the time of flight of the bullet combined—these affect the point ahead of the aircraft, at which bullets have to be directed in order to meet the aircraft in their flight.

The direction of flight of the aircraft—this affects the apparent position of the point at which the bullets have to be directed, or, in other words, it affects the amount of deflection required.

Deflection may be upward, downward, or lateral, or a combination of either of the first two with the latter.

Most of the above-mentioned factors are ever changing, so that it is not practicable to use "range-finding," "angle of sight" or other instruments.

TABLES OF ALLOWANCES.

It is possible to determine by calculation the correct elevation and deflection required to hit aircraft under any given combination of the following:—Distance, speed, angle of sight and direction of flight.

From these calculated results "tables of allowances" can be compiled, but as the distance of an aircraft from the gun may frequently vary as much as a mile in a minute it is obvious that "tables" based on "distances" are not satisfactory to work on.

It has been found that "tables" derived from the above are far more simple when the "altitude" is considered instead of the "distance."

Opportunities of firing at aircraft with small arms are sudden and fleeting, so that the use of lengthy "tables" when firing is out of the question even if an approximate estimate could be formed of the speed and altitude of aircraft.

An examination of "tables of allowances" shows that certain sighting elevations and deflections remain fairly constant as the changing conditions of some of the above-mentioned factors counteract each other. It is therefore possible to use one table only, designed to apply to average conditions, and to ensure that the cone of fire will in nearly all cases envelop the hostile machine.

APPROXIMATE AVERAGE CONDITIONS AT WHICH FIRE FROM SMALL ARMS MAY BE EXPECTED TO BE EFFECTIVE.

SPEED.—The average speed of aircraft in still air may be taken as *approximately 80 miles per hour.*

ANGLE OF SIGHT.—Aircraft at a reasonable height if at a small angle of sight must naturally be at a very considerable distance, whilst aircraft almost immediately overhead are not the rule. The ordinary angle of sight therefore would vary from about 30° to 70°, so *the average may be taken as approximately 50°.*

DISTANCE.—Experience has proved that aircraft at over 3,000 feet altitude are practically invulnerable. An aeroplane at that height and at the average angle of sight (50°) is 1,300 yards from the gun, which according to a German document is the limit of distance at which there is any prospect of success. As aircraft seldom approach very near the Gun, we may take the *useful average as 2,000 feet altitude*, or about 900 yards distance at an angle of sight of 50°.

DIRECTION OF FLIGHT.—We need only consider the following eight general directions :—

Coming—Going—Crossing to right or left.

Coming and crossing diagonally to right or left.

Going and crossing diagonally to right or left.

SIMPLIFIED TABLE.—(80.M.P.H., 2,000 feet altitude, Angle of Sight 50°).

Taking these averages we get the following simple table of elevations and deflections :—

DIRECTION OF FLIGHT.

Coming	Coming and crossing diagonally		Crossing		Going and crossing diagonally		Going
Elevation	Elevation	Deflection	Elevation	Deflection	Elevation	Deflection	Elevation
4°·15′	3°	3°	0°·30′	4°·20′	−2°·30′	3°·10′	−3°·20′

NECESSITY FOR A SPECIAL SIGHT.

Even this simplified table necessitates :—

Five separate sighting elevations, of which two are below Zero and cannot be set with the ordinary sight, and three amounts of deflection to either side.

Alterations of sight adjustment waste valuable time, and it is impossible for anyone to judge the necessary allowances when " aiming off " an aircraft moving at high speed.

To overcome these difficulties it is necessary to have a special back-sight giving the required sight setting for any of the above directions of flight.

A back sight of this description having eight large apertures, one applicable to each direction of flight, enables the firer to aim *at* the aircraft with no other distraction than that of changing to the correct aperture at each change of direction of the aircraft, this change of aperture is simplified by the use of transparent material for the sight.

The back sight must be fixed on the Gun in the same position as the tangent sight.

A special high fore-sight must be used in conjunction with a back sight of this description to allow of the depression necessary under certain conditions being obtained.

The fore sight must be of such a height above the ordinary fore sight that a line from the Zero of the A.A. back sight to the tip of the special fore sight is parallel to a line from the tangent sight *set at zero* to the tip of the ordinary fore sight.

DIMENSIONS IN INCHES OF SPECIAL A.A. BACK SIGHT FOR VICKERS OR MAXIM GUNS.—Sight radius 36 inches.

```
                          + 2·76

          + 1·94                        + 1·94
        Left 1·94                     Right 1·94
+  ·35                   +  ·26                      +  ·35
Left 2·76                  *                      Right 2·76
          − 1·60                        − 1·60
        Left 2·00                     Right 2·00

                          − 2·15
```

DIMENSIONS IN INCHES OF SPECIAL A.A. BACK SIGHT FOR LEWIS GUNS.—Sight Radius 32 inches.

```
                          + 2·46

          + 1·72                        + 1·72
        Left 1·72                     Right 1·72
+  ·31                   +  ·23                      +  ·31
Left 2·46                  *                      Right 2·46
          − 1·42                        − 1·42
        Left 1·79                     Right 1·79

                          − 1·90
```

Measurements show the distance of the centre of each aperture from Zero, which is shown by an *. Apertures should be $\frac{5}{16}$ths of an inch in diameter.

The centre aperture gives a fixed sight for approximately 500 yards.

METHOD OF USING THE SIGHT.

The aperture to be used against aircraft in each direction of flight is as follows :—

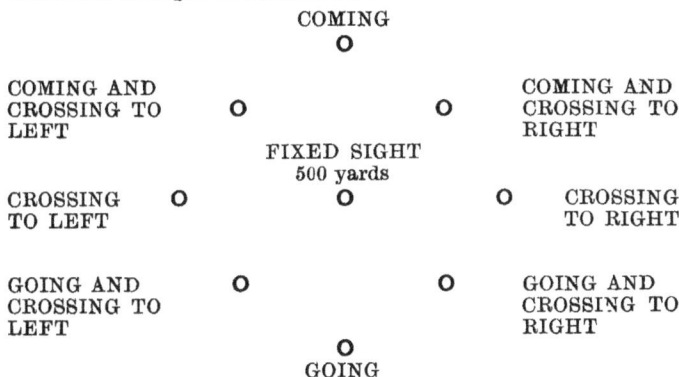

	COMING	
	O	
COMING AND CROSSING TO LEFT	O O	COMING AND CROSSING TO RIGHT
	FIXED SIGHT 500 yards	
CROSSING O TO LEFT	O	O CROSSING TO RIGHT
GOING AND O CROSSING TO LEFT	O	GOING AND CROSSING TO RIGHT
	O	
	GOING	

The fixed sight (centre aperture) should be used against an aeroplane diving straight at the gun, with the object of firing at it with a fixed gun.

Should the firer at any time be in doubt which aperture to use he should bring the aircraft roughly into the centre of the whole sight, the aperture towards which the aircraft then appears to be flying is the correct one.

For fire to be effective it is essential that it should be maintained continuously throughout the whole time that it is considered that there is a reasonable chance of hitting the aircraft, otherwise a pause may occur in the firing just at the moment when the maximum effect is being produced. It is not necessary to cease fire when changing from one aperture to another.

To enable fire to be continuous a suitable anti-aircraft mounting is necessary for Machine and Lewis guns as well as a belt holder for machine guns.

The difficulty of maintaining the aim on an aircraft, and the vibration of the gun which is only supported by the mounting at one point, makes the cone of fire considerably larger than that obtained under normal conditions; this fact increases the chance of success.

HIGH ANGLE SMALL ARM BARRAGE FIRE AGAINST AIRCRAFT.

It is frequently suggested that aircraft should be made to pass through a "cone" of small arm fire. This can sometimes be done when the aircraft is coming directly towards, or going directly away, from the Gun, but if the aircraft forms a crossing target, there is no means of ensuring that the "cone" is not over or under it. When it is considered that the aircraft has passed through the barrage the cone is moved so that it may have to pass through again.

Even when the aircraft passes through the cone of fire it must be realized that at an average speed it travels over four yards in the space of time separating any two consecutive bullets, even from a Lewis Gun; therefore very few bullets from one gun can arrive during the time taken by the aircraft in passing through the cone.

It is therefore clear that there is little chance of damaging aircraft by "barrage" fire from small arms, when using the ordinary sights, except in the case of a direct "Coming" or "Going" target, and even then only when a considerable number of weapons are available; a combination which is seldom likely to occur.

Even in the case of "Coming" or "Going" targets there is the difficulty of knowing when to commence and when to stop the barrage, or in other words, we come back to a modification of some of the original difficulties :—

(i.) To judge the maximum and minimum upward deflection in the case of "Coming" targets, and the maximum and minium downward deflection in the case of "Going" targets, because outside the maximum and minimum limits it is of no use firing.

(ii.) The estimation of these limits when aiming off.

A special sight could be made for use in barrage fire on the principle of that already described, and could be used not only for " Coming " and " Going " targets, but also for those moving in different directions.

The difference between the application of fire when using the two sights would be :—

(1) WITH THE A.A. SIGHT, the centre of the cone of fire is applied constantly in the vicinity of the aeroplane, admittedly sometimes in front, or behind, and above or below, or right or left, with the probability that some part of the cone envelopes the target.

(2) WITH THE A.A. BARRAGE SIGHT, the cone of fire would be applied sufficiently far in front of the aircraft to allow of the necessary deflection for the fastest aircraft at say 8,000 feet, and kept steady till the necessary deflection for the slowest aircraft at a low altitude was reached, the gun being then traversed back slowly or quickly till the maximum deflection was again reached, and so on, similarly the cone would be sometimes above or below, or right or left, and during each stop and forward traverse would be either in front or behind except for a few moments.

In practice, owing to the vibration of the gun and the difficulty of maintaining the aim, etc., there would probably be sufficient irregularities in the application of the cone with the A.A. Sight to approach the effect produced by using the A.A. Barrage Sight, but the extreme cases would not be included, and the probability is that, considering the law of averages, the former sight would be most generally efficient.

HORIZONTAL BARRAGE FIRE WITH SMALL ARMS.

It is sometimes suggested that aircraft may be engaged from the ground by applying a cone of fire which in part is parallel to, and coincident with, the line of flight. This is only possible when the aircraft is immediately approaching towards, or going away from the gun. From the trajectory tables of the Vickers Gun it can be seen that an aircraft travelling in either of these directions, and maintaining certain very low altitudes, will be in the cone of fire between certain distances from the Gun.

7

These distances are shown in the following theoretical table:—

Altitude (maintained by aircraft).	Distances from the Gun between which Aircraft is in Cone of Fire considering probable depth of the Cone.		Quadrant elevation of the Gun.	
	Approximate only.		Degrees.	Minutes.
50 feet	600 to 1,100 yards	...	1	57
100 ,,	750 to 1,300 ,,	...	2	57
150 ,,	900 to 1,400 ,,	...	3	47
200 ,,	1,000 to 1,500 ,,	...	4	48
250 ,,	1,100 to 1,600 ,,	...	5	22
300 ,,	1,200 to 1,700 ,,	...	6	—
350 ,,	1,250 to 1,750 ,,	...	6	41
400 ,,	1,300 to 1,800 ,,	...	7	27
450 ,,	1,350 to 1,850 ,,	...	8	16
500 ,,	1,400 to 1,900 ,,			
550 ,,	1,450 to 1,950 ,,	...	9	11
600 ,,	1,500 to 2,000 ,,			
650 ,,	1,525 to 2,025 ,,	...	10	10
700 ,,	1,575 to 2,075 ,,			
750 ,,	1,600 to 2,100 ,,	...	11	15

Theoretically to obtain effect by *aiming at* the aircraft between the above limits at each altitude, the sighting of the gun should vary between approximately 200 yards less than the shorter distance, and 100 yards less than the longer distance. Taking the mean range for each altitude, the sighting varies from 700 yards for an altitude of 50 feet to 1,700 yards at 750 feet.

As it is impracticable to find the correct altitude, or to alter sights, the mean of the whole could be taken as 1,200 yards, and the gun could be given a slight upward and downward movement of about 1 degree either way—that is, to about half a finger's width above and below the aircraft.

It is clear from the above that the aircraft can only be subjected to this "horizontal barrage" whilst it is inside the limits shown approximately by the figure A B C D, a great deal of which is beyond the limit of 1,300 yards, within which effective fire may be expected.

8

DRAWN TO SCALE V.I. 50 FEET

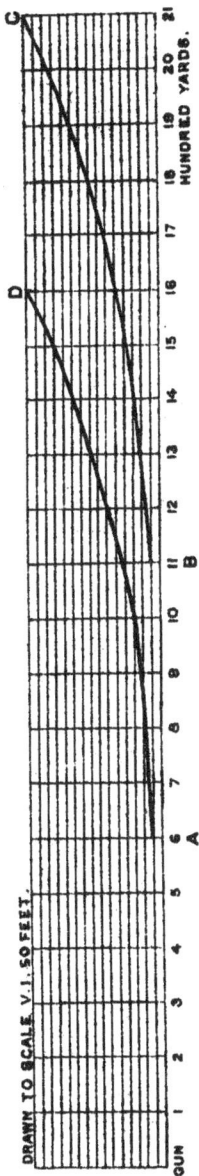

The distance D C would be far less than the distance A B were it not for the fact that a cone of fire increases considerably in depth as the range increases.

The width of this figure would average approximately 10 yards. As the aircraft gets further from the limits of this figure it comes within the ordinary conditions of anti-aircraft fire. As the angle of the gun position to point " D " from the horizontal is only a little over 9 degrees, the aircraft, when within the limits of the figure never appears to be more than " *one hand's width above the horizon,*" so that the cases when this method could be used by day would be extremely rare, particularly when it is remembered that the direction of flight must be directly towards, or away from, the gun.

This method might be of use for the protection of an absolutely straight, long and narrow Dump, etc., where VERY LOW flying aircraft might be expected—for example, at night where a road might give the "line" and would only be visible from an altitude of a few hundred feet —one or more guns could be laid for direction (considering wind allowances), and by a system of stops be prevented from moving vertically beyond the limits of quadrant elevations of 2 and 11 degrees. As the aircraft would be invisible at night, the guns would have to search between these limits.

Very special precautions would be necessary when using a " horizontal barrage " to prevent damage to friendly troops in the danger zone.

9

WIND.

Wind affects both the flight of aircraft and of the bullets; in the former case it has a very great effect on the speed with relation to the ground, but in various degrees according to the direction of flight, in the latter case in an ever increasing proportion to the time of flight of the bullet. This, though increasing the difficulty of introducing a theoretically perfect method of engaging aircraft with small arm fire, does not materially alter the chance of obtaining effect by working on the principle of averages.

RIFLE FIRE.

Owing to the greater dispersion of rifle fire as compared to machine gun and Lewis gun fire, the former would probably be the most effective against aircraft, but a large number of rifles is necessary to obtain sufficient volume, and these are not always available when or where required.

A special A.A. rifle sight could be made on the same principle as that for the Machine and Lewis Gun, but would necessarily have a short "sight radius" to prevent strain on the neck, and to enable the firer to use the various apertures without excessive movement of the head.

When a special sight is not available, the following ROUGH GUIDE will be useful when firing at an aeroplane flying at and maintaining about 2,000 feet altitude :—

DIRECTION OF FLIGHT.	SIGHTING ELEVATION.	POINT OF AIM.
Coming	2000	AT the Aeroplane.
Coming and crossing diagonally	1700	1½ fingers to RIGHT or LEFT according to direction of flight.
Crossing	600	2 fingers in FRONT of Aeroplane.
Going and crossing	Zero	1½ fingers between {4 & 5} {7 & 8} o'clock of the aeroplane, according to direction of flight.
Going	Zero	1½ fingers BELOW the aeroplane.

Firing must be carefully controlled,

TRACER AMMUNITION.

Contemplated improvements in this type of ammunition may facilitate firing at aircraft by rendering observation and correction of fire possible, but observation of tracer bullets in the air is often very deceptive and requires considerable practice.

THEORETICAL CONSIDERATIONS BEARING ON TACTICAL CONSIDERATIONS.

Theoretically, considering both what are considered by the British and Germans as the limits at which small arm fire is effective against aircraft, Sketch 1 shews that one gun can only effectively cover a circle of 800 yards radius at an altitude of 3,000 feet. So that if it is desired to bring effective fire to bear on an aircraft at that altitude when passing over any particular spot, the gun should not be further from that point than 800 yards.

SKETCH 1. SECTIONAL ELEVATION.

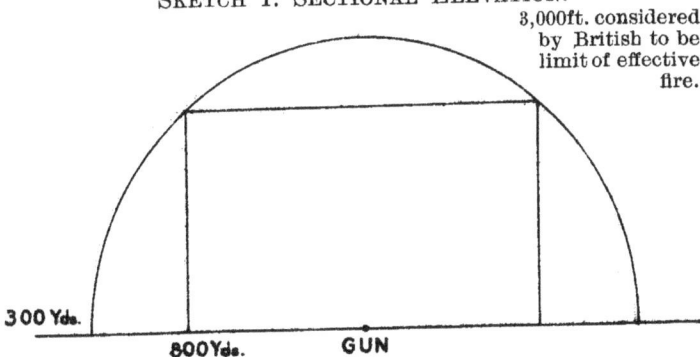

3,000ft. considered by British to be limit of effective fire.

3 00 Yds.

800 Yds.　　　　GUN

Considered by Germans to be limit of effective fire.

SKETCH 2 (a, b and c) gives three special cases in which guns are placed at various distances apart with a view to covering a definite line "A" with a belt of effective A.A. Fire up to an altitude of 3,000 feet. It is clear that as the guns are placed closer together, so the effective belt becomes more uniform in width, consequently the gun positions can be placed further from that line, provided they do not exceed 800 yards.

11

The closer the guns are together the more guns are within effective range of aircraft crossing the line.

(a)

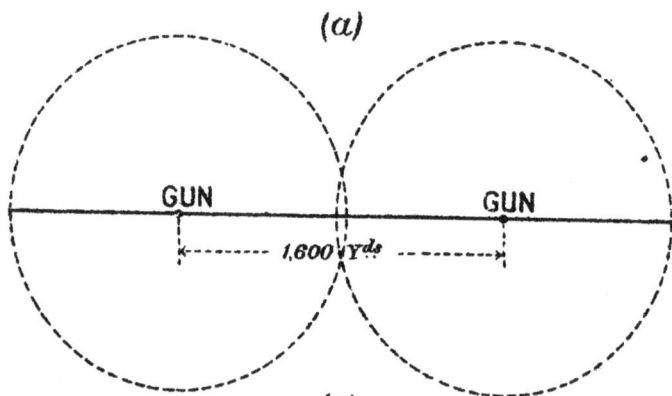

GUN   GUN

←------- 1,600 Yᵈˢ -------→

(b)

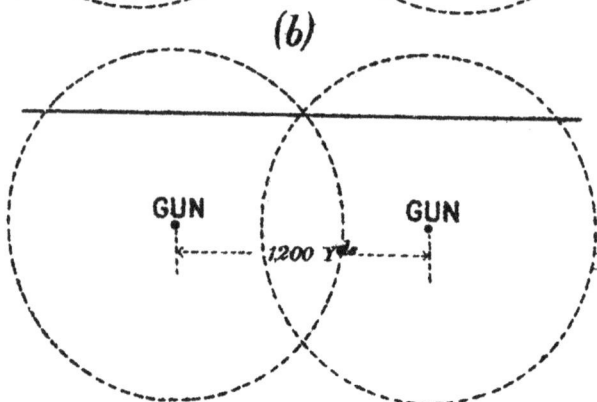

GUN   GUN

←---- 1,200 Yᵈˢ ----→

(c)

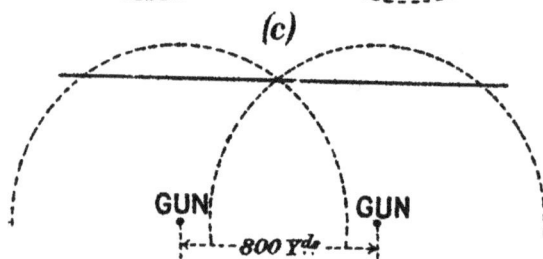

GUN   GUN

←--- 800 Yᵈˢ ---→

12

TACTICAL CONSIDERATIONS.

Small arm fire from the ground can never form a substitute for the action of our own aircraft or for anti-aircraft gun fire against hostile machines, but it does form a very useful addition to those means of attack. It is not always possible to count on our own aeroplanes being in the right place at the right time, and to A.A. guns the low flying aeroplane forms the most difficult of targets.

The main uses of small arm fire in anti-aircraft work are :—

(a) The prevention of efficient work by hostile "contact aeroplanes."

(b) The immediate protection of areas such as dumps, aerodromes, etc.

(c) The protection of kite balloons.

(d) Action against low flying scouts.

As regards (a):—It is suggested that this is best carried out by Machine guns or Lewis guns placed in fixed positions in the line. The interval between the guns is limited by the number of guns available for this work, but it is not desirable for them to be more than 1,000 yards apart, nor for them to be more than 1,000 yards from the first line. The position of these guns must be carefully concealed. As their object is to prevent efficient work by scaring the enemy, fire should be opened by all guns within range so as to keep the hostile planes too far off or too high to do their work.

SKETCH 3. PLAN.

Method of forming a belt of effective A.A. Machine Gun or Lewis Gun Fire.

Belt of effective A.A. Machine Gun or Lewis Gun Fire

As regards (b) :—The guns should be distributed over the area at intervals according to their number, so that effective fire may be brought to bear on such enemy aircraft as may suddenly appear at a low altitude to drop bombs, whilst others at a considerable altitude are engaging the attention of A.A. guns or our aeroplanes. Gun detachments should be warned of this method of attack. Again the object is to keep the hostile machines away, all guns within range should therefore immediately open fire.

As regards (c) :—In this case the object to be protected may itself be at a considerable altitude, even greater than that at which machine gun fire may be expected to be effective, but fire must be opened immediately the hostile plane is within range with a view to keeping it away. Great care will be necessary to avoid hitting the balloon.

The guns should be placed where it is least likely that they will be masked by the balloon or cable; they should be sufficiently close to afford immediate protection to the balloon.

The gun positions must be carefully concealed, as the attacker will endeavour to keep the balloon between himself and the gun.

As regards (d) :—If the gun is not actually detailed for the protection of a particular object, or performing a specific duty as in (a), its object will be to bring down the hostile machine, not to scare it away; for this purpose fire should be withheld till the target is within *effective* range.

The struts of an aeroplane almost invariably become visible to the naked eye at a distance of between 1,300 and 1,600 yards.

PRECAUTIONS.

When Machine Guns are used for firing at aircraft the barrel casing must contain as much water as possible. This can be ensured when filling, by tilting the muzzle downwards and turning the gun slightly over to the left, so that the filling hole is at the highest point. The filling hole plug should be replaced before levelling the gun, and the cork plug should remain in as long as possible.

If the barrel casing is not full the gun must be frequently levelled, so that the water may reach the fore part of the barrel. If this is not done barrels will be rendered unserviceable.

Very special safety precautions are necessary in arranging for and using a Horizontal Barrage. Dimensions of danger areas are given in Musketry Regulations, Part II.

Rifle and Machine Gun Fire against any airship is absolutely prohibited, unless the airship has revealed its hostile character unmistakably by dropping bombs (G.H.Q. letter O.B./147 of June, '16.)

Troops should on no account fire at an aeroplane unless the German Black Cross is distinctly visible. (S.S. 350 dated 1916.) But as it is important that hostile aeroplanes should be recognised as far off as possible, Vickers and Lewis gunners should be instructed in the recognition of aeroplanes at long ranges.

www.ingramcontent.com/pod-product-compliance
Lightning Source LLC
Chambersburg PA
CBHW020953030426
42339CB00004B/82